Mickey's Magnet

by FRANKLYN M. BRANLEY
and
ELEANOR K. VAUGHAN

Pictures by Crockett Johnson

SCHOLASTIC BOOK SERVICES

NEW YORK · TORONTO · LONDON · AUCKLAND · SYDNEY

ISBN: 0-590-02334-9

Text Copyright © 1956 by Franklyn M. Branley and Eleanor K. Vaughan. Illustrations copyright © 1956 by Crockett Johnson. This edition is published by Scholastic Book Services, a division of Scholastic Magazines, Inc., by arrangement with Thomas Y. Crowell Company.

28 27 26 25 24 23 22   2 3 4 5 6/8

07

Printed in the U.S.A.

Here is Mickey, looking at a picture book.

He hears his mother speaking. She wants a box of pins.

Mickey leaves his book and gets the box of pins. He runs to give them to his mother.

Whoops! He trips on the rug. The
pins scatter all over the floor —
some in the cracks,
some on the rug,
and some on the big blue
chair. What a mess!

Mickey starts to pick them up. One pin. Two pins. Now three at a time.

This is slow work. Perhaps a spoon would be quicker.

One spoonful. Two spoonfuls. Not much quicker.

"Maybe a horseshoe magnet will help."

Mickey looks up. His father hands him something heavy.

This could *help?*

But how? Would it push the pins into a pile?

He'd try it and see.

Wow! Pins are all over the ends of the magnet. He doesn't even have to push them together.

"Here you are!" he says to his mother.

He shakes the magnet. A few pins fall into his mother's lap. The others hang onto the magnet. He has to pull them off.

This is fun! He'll get some more.

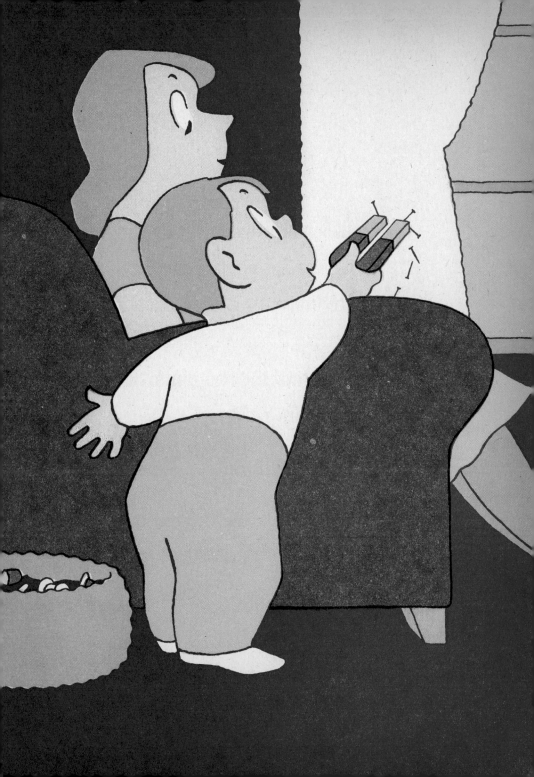

He rubs the magnet over the rug. He moves it along the crack in the floor. He pushes it across the big blue chair.

Now he has all the pins. He fills the box again.

He'd like to keep on spilling them. But his mother needs her pins.

He sees her sewing basket. It is full of things —

scissors and buttons,

needles and thread,

a plastic thimble,

a bunch of hooks.

He pushes the magnet into the basket.

Up come the scissors, needles, and hooks.

No buttons? No thread? No thimble? The magnet seems to pick up only metal.

He takes the scissors, needles, and hooks, and looks around for other things to pick up.

He tries

a china cat,

a small glass dish,

a piece of silver paper,

and a smooth, round stone.

The magnet picks up none of them.

He'd better look for something else.

What can he find in the kitchen?
    —a bent bottle cap,
    a piece of white soap,
    and a nice shiny penny.
How about that rubber bone on
the floor beside Rusty's bowl?
Mickey squats down. He drops
everything.
    Plop goes the bottle cap.
    Plop goes the penny.
    Right into the water!

Perhaps the magnet will lift them out.

Up comes the bottle cap. But not the penny.

He tries again. Still no penny.

He has to take it out with his fingers.

The magnet won't even pick it up from his hand. Magnets won't pick up pennies, dry or wet! But aren't pennies made of metal?

Mickey can't understand. But his father will know.

Together they try
    a dime,
    a quarter,
    an aluminum candy dish.

"A magnet attracts only iron and steel. It won't pick up other metals," says his father.

Mickey touches the magnet to a painted wooden horse. Nothing happens. How about a lead soldier? No iron or steel here!

He sits down to play with his collection. First he picks up the needle with a magnet. A pin is hanging from the needle.

The needle must be a magnet, too!

He pulls the needle off the magnet. Down drops the pin.

He tries to pick it up with the needle. Nothing happens.

So now it isn't a magnet!

Again he picks up the needle with the magnet and touches the pin. The needle picks up the pin.

"Look," he says to his father. "Sometimes the needle's a magnet."

"Yes," says Father, "and watch this." Mickey counts as his father rubs a needle along the horseshoe magnet. Five times . . . ten times . . . twenty times.

Now the needle picks up the pin.

"A magnet!" cries Mickey. "It picks up the pin! I want to make a magnet, too."

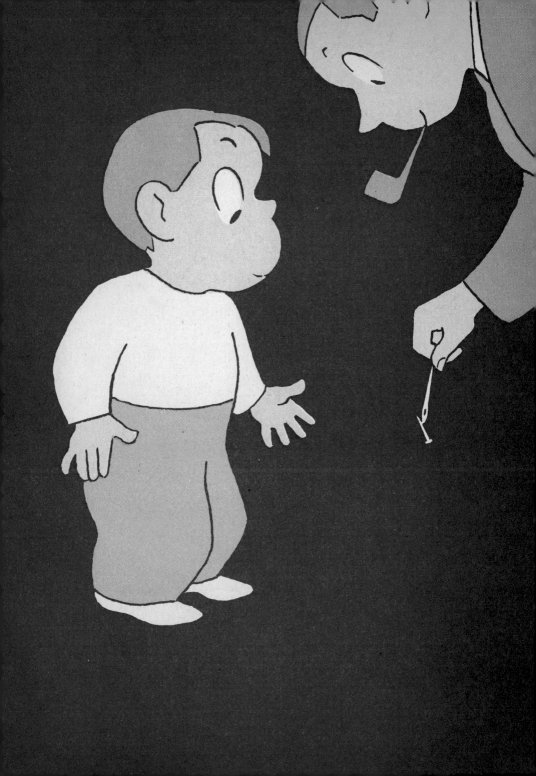

He takes another needle. He rubs it and rubs it and rubs it, always in the same direction, along the horseshoe magnet.

It works!

"Look, I made a magnet." He runs to his mother. Oh-h-h-h ... There goes the box of pins. Pins all over the floor again.

He starts to pick them up.
But it's easy this time. He has a
magnet.

A magnet Mickey made himself.

Here is a magnet you can use. It is called a bar magnet. There are other kinds of magnets, too.

Mickey picked up pins with a horseshoe magnet. Can you pick up pins with your bar magnet? Use your magnet to do some of the things that Mickey did.

What else can you find out about your new magnet?